Dear

YOU WERE NEVER MEANT
TO WANDER IN THE DARK

Truthseeker

Grace Abbey

Published by:
R.H. Publishing
Dallas, Texas
www.rhpublishingcompany.com

Copyright © 2025, Grace Abbey

ISBN#978-1-960494-35-1

DEDICATION

I dedicate this book to the Truth, Himself—Jesus Christ, my Savior, King, and Friend, Who taught me to love, trust, and embrace suffering, not as punishment, but as a testimony to the power of His resurrection. Through it, the victory He won on the cross, has become my daily victory, helping me overcome and walk in freedom.

ACKNOWLEDGMENTS

To my Lord and Savior, Jesus Christ—thank You for rescuing me, redeeming me, and never letting go. You are the reason I live, the reason I write, and the reason this message matters.

To my daughter, Kamillah, for designing the book cover. Watching you grow into the woman God created you to be gives me joy beyond words. Your life is a testament of grace and purpose. Thank you for your love, patience, and encouragement through every season.

To my faithful friends who prayed, dreamed, and believed with me—from the early days of Friday night prayer meetings to the birth of the Mansfield House of Prayer—you know who you are. Thank you for sharing this journey with me.

To my spiritual mom, the pastors and leaders at Gateway Church, Kenneth Copeland Ministries, and the US Army Reserve, thank you for investing in me, trusting me, and creating spaces where truth and freedom can flourish.

To the city of Mansfield, Texas, thank you for providing a place for prayer, worship, and community to grow. May the intercession rising from this city echo through generations to come.

To every Truthseeker who picks up this book—you're the reason I wrote it. My prayer is that as you turn each page, you'll hear the Father's voice calling you closer. May you come to know the Truth, not just as an idea, but as a Person. And may you never be the same.

All glory to God. For the audience of One.

FOREWORD

Grace is a woman who takes God's word to heart. As a single mom and prayer warrior, she has contended for God's provision and promises to come to pass in her life. And, guess what?! They have! She stands as a witness to many, declaring with conviction, "This is the way! Go in it." Her words are not only wise but urgent, echoing a deep spiritual truth that resonates with those seeking freedom and purpose.

In a world filled with countless paths and choices, Grace points to the One sure and good path that leads to wisdom. Her voice is a clarion call, inviting us to listen with our spiritual ears to the guidance of the Holy Spirit, who speaks in the depths of our hearts.

I've had the privilege of knowing Grace for many years, both as a ministry partner and a dear friend. Her commitment to personal freedom and spiritual growth is unwavering. With each new revelation and discovery, Grace turns to those around her—in life and now through the pages of this book—urging them to follow the path she has found. "This is the way! Go in it," she says, not as a mere suggestion, but as a heartfelt plea born out of experience and a divine encounter. Her journey has been marked by perseverance, faith, and a relentless pursuit of truth. She reminds us that our work—the work of resting—is vital. It is through our own surrender that we are transformed into beacons of hope for others.

Grace's advocacy for inner freedom is deeply practical and rooted in her own life story. She has led a citywide House of Prayer, taught college courses on spiritual identity and freedom, and mentored countless individuals, including her own daughter, who has now grown into a woman of faith.

Grace's dedication to helping others discover their identity in Christ as Beloved is the heartbeat of this book. She believes, with every fiber of her being, that we are already given this identity—it is not something to earn, but something to realize.

If you've ever struggled to see yourself as Beloved, if you've ever questioned your worth or wondered about your purpose, the book you hold in your hands may be the answer you've been searching for. Grace's words are more than encouragement: they are a roadmap. She invites you to walk with her, to explore the truths she has uncovered, and to experience the freedom that comes from knowing who you truly are in Christ.

Her message is clear and consistent:
> "This is the way! Go in it."

Elizabeth Settle
Co-Founder of SettledCo and Settled Foundation
www.settledco.com

TABLE OF CONTENTS

Introduction 13

1. **The Search Begins** 15
   Why your questions matter, and why your longing
   for more is not a weakness but a signal that you
   were made for something real.

2. **When Truth Feels Like a Moving Target** 21
   Exposing the lie of relative truth and the confusion
   it brings.

3. **The Truth That Stands Alone** 31
   Understanding absolute truth through the person
   of Jesus Christ.

4. **A Hope You Can't Manufacture** 43
   Why the world's version of hope eventually crumbles, and
   how biblical hope endures.

5. **The Way, the Truth, and the Life** 51
   Breaking down John 14:6 and what it means that
   Jesus is the only way.

6. **Religion vs. Relationship** 57
   How the truth of Jesus sets you free from legalism, shame,
   and performance.

7. **Truth That Confronts and Heals** 67
   What happens when God's truth exposes the lies we've
   believed, and begins to restore us.

8. **Hope in the Middle of the Mess** 79
    Learning to trust the unshakable truth of God when life
    feels like chaos.

9. **What It Means to Follow the Truth** 87
    Discipleship, surrender, and living a life grounded
    in the unchanging Word of God.

10. **An Invitation to Come Home** 95
    A personal call to accept the Truth, receive real hope, and
    begin walking in purpose with Jesus.

INTRODUCTION

WHY BOTHER?

"If God is sovereign and the ultimate decider of all things, then why bother trying to please Him or do better? You might feel the odds are stacked against you, and nothing you do matters. So, why bother?"

These were the thoughts and questions that once plagued a teenager; we will read about him later in the chapters, that everything is already decided, and he gets nothing. But what he didn't consider was the Truth himself.

The apostle John writes:
>*"I have no greater joy than this, to hear that my spiritual children are living their lives in Truth"*
(3 John 1:4, NKJV).

Your longing and your questions matter deeply. They are not a weakness. They signal that you were made for something real, something eternal, and can only be found in the pursuit of Truth. The One you have not yet *known* calls out to you.

So, Truthseeker, let's begin this journey together.

Chapter 1

The Search Begins

Dear Truthseeker,

Why do your questions matter? Why is your longing for more not a weakness but a signal that you were made for something real?

I still remember the moment when the words echoed in my spirit: *"Write it now; write it with diligence."* I paused and asked, "Write what, Lord?" I knew who I was writing to: Truthseekers like you, I knew why I needed to write, but the clarity about what to write was still hazy. Then I heard the gentle assurance of the Holy Spirit: *"I am here to help."*

Truthseeker, this is what it's all about. In my thirty-eight years of walking with Christ, it never occurred to me to write a book. Until the moment I felt an urgency, a divine push to write a love letter to those He is pursuing: Truthseekers.
I realized my desire to know Jesus deeply and to disciple others into that intimacy was not unique; it was urgent and necessary. Many have been called to this mission, but some turned it into a ministry for fame, aiming to be influencers rather than to influence.

The Lord spoke to me clearly:
"I am looking for the one who just wants Me and will not exploit the assignment."

I was given dreams meant for those with many "followers." I shared these dreams with people I thought would steward them, but they dismissed them. I wondered, *"Can't they see what You are telling them through this dream?"*

Then, one morning, I awoke to these words:
"I gave the dream to you. It has an appointed time. I will raise you as a voice to the nations, and this dream will be a catalyst to reveal Me to the Truthseekers. Write it now; write it with diligence."

This reminded me of John the Revelator, who received instructions on the island of Patmos to write what is now known as the last book of the Bible, the Revelation of Jesus Christ.

He wrote,
> "I was once in the Spirit on the Lord's Day, and behind me, I heard a great voice like a war trumpet, saying: 'I am the Alpha and Omega, the First and the Last. Write promptly what you see (your vision) in a book and send it to the seven churches'"
(Revelation 1:8,10-11, ESV).

In this search, one of the most important truths to understand is that your desire for more is not a flaw or a failure; it's part of who you were made to be. You were created for a purpose, for a relationship that satisfies your deepest longings.

In this search, one of the most important truths to understand is that your desire for more is not a flaw or a failure; it's part of who you were made to be. You were created for a purpose, for a relationship that satisfies your deepest longings.

Sometimes, the journey can feel confusing or overwhelming.

In a world filled with shifting ideas of what's true, you might wonder if there even *is* a truth to find. Maybe you've felt disappointed by answers that don't satisfy, or you've encountered voices claiming to have the Truth but only leading you astray. I want to assure you: the search is worth it. Your questions matter, and your heart's desire for meaning is a beacon guiding you toward the One who alone holds all Truth.

How to Begin
A Prayer for the One Who's Just Beginning

God of all Truth,

I don't know everything, and I'm finally okay admitting that. I want to believe You are real not just in theory, but in presence. Not just a doctrine, but a Person.

If You are the Truth, show me. Open my ears to Your voice and open my heart to Your pursuit. Forgive me for the ways I've sought answers in everything but You. And give me the courage to follow, even when it means letting go of the familiar.

This is me answering the knock. I don't know the whole path, but I trust that you will walk it with me.
Amen.

This journey starts with a willingness to seek honestly and openly. It requires courage to ask the hard questions and the patience to wait for answers that may not come all at once. But most importantly, it needs a heart that's open to being changed.

In my own life, I have learned that seeking Truth isn't about having all the answers immediately. It's about moving forward even when the path is unclear; it's about trusting that the One Who made you also wants to reveal Himself to you.

Jesus said,

> *"You will seek me and find me when you seek me*
> *with all your heart"* (Jeremiah 29:13, ESV).

This is an invitation to seek not just facts or rules, but a relationship with God, a relationship that changes everything.

This is just the beginning. Welcome to the search.
This journey began because you dared to ask, *"Is there more?"* That question is not a weakness. It's evidence of your design. You were made to seek, to knock, and to discover Truth that satisfies, not just pacifies.

What to Expect
Along this journey, you will encounter moments of clarity and moments of doubt. There will be times when the pieces fall into place and others when the puzzle feels impossible. That's all part of the process.

I want you to know you are not alone in this. Many before you have walked this path, wrestling with questions and longing for answers. The difference is that the Truth you seek is not hidden or unreachable; Truth is alive and wants to be known by you.

This book is a letter to you, a fellow *Truthseeker*. It is my prayer that as you read it, you will be encouraged, challenged, and equipped to keep moving forward. Because your pursuit matters. Your story matters. And the Truth is worth it.

The Invitation to Keep Seeking
Your journey has already begun simply because you've asked the questions and allowed yourself to long for something more. That longing is a gift, a compass pointing you toward your Creator, Who knows you intimately and loves you deeply.

As you continue reading, I encourage you to keep your heart open, your mind curious, and your spirit courageous. There will be moments that challenge what you think you know, moments that stretch your faith, and moments that fill you with hope and peace.

Remember, seeking Truth is not a race or a checklist. It's a lifelong adventure with a guide who never leaves your side. The One Who is the Alpha and Omega, the Beginning and the End, is ready to meet you wherever you are.

So, take a deep breath, settle your heart, and prepare to journey deeper. The Truth you seek is closer than you think.

> *"Come to me, all who are weary and burdened, and I will give you rest"* (Matthew 11:28, NKJV).

Personal Challenge to the Truthseeker
This week, take one step toward deeper honesty with God. Set aside 10 minutes each day to ask yourself:
"What am I really searching for?"

Write it down without censoring yourself. Don't try to sound holy; just be real. Let your search begin in Truth.
Be honest about your hunger. What are you chasing?

Validation? Success? Belonging? Bring that ache into the light and ask, *"What am I truly seeking?"*

Write it down.
- Write a letter. Yes, write a letter to God. Tell Him what you want to believe, what you're afraid of, and what you hope is true. This isn't for performance. It's for honesty. And that's where the real Truth begins.

- Notice the pursuit. Look for signs this week that God is already pursuing you. A conversation. A scripture. A moment of peace you can't explain. He is not far off. He is near, even now.

You are not alone in your seeking. And you are not the only one being called. The invitation to Truth is loud, clear, and deeply personal.

Prayer

"Father,

I confess that I've often searched for meaning in things that do not satisfy. I want to know You, not just ideas about You. Speak to me in the stillness. Guide my thoughts, my questions, and my longings. Show me how to trust that You are already pursuing me. Amen."

Journal Prompt
Where in my life do I sense a longing for something more? What is that longing pointing me toward?

_____

_____

_____

_____

_____

_____

_____

_____

Scripture Reflection
Jeremiah 29:13,
"You will seek me and find me when you seek me with all your heart" (ESV).

Chapter 2

When Truth Feels Like a
Moving Target

Dear Truthseeker,

**Have you ever felt like the truth keeps slipping through
your fingers?** One moment, you're convinced of what's
right, and the next, a new voice, a new argument, or a new
crisis throws everything into question. In today's culture,
"truth" often feels more like a trend than a foundation. Is truth
constantly shifting, evolving, or up for debate?

Truth is not a theory. Truth is not a trend. Truth is a Person and
that changes everything.

Maybe that's where you are now. Maybe you've asked
questions like:
- *If God is sovereign, why even try?*
- *Why does it feel like I can never get ahead?*
- *Why should I bother when nothing seems to
  change?*

The teenager, I referenced earlier, asked me, "If God already
knows everything and decides everything, then what's the point
of trying? I still lose." His words weren't disrespectful. They
were raw and honest. Beneath his frustration was a deep ache
for meaning and hope. What he hadn't yet considered was The
Truth Himself.

What he didn't realize is that even in the way he framed the question, he was already carrying a certain picture of God in his mind. To him, God looked like a distant dictator, someone who predetermines outcomes, leaves no room for freedom, and sets us up to fail. If that's Who God is, then of course life feels like a rigged game.

Our conception of Him shapes our hope, choices, and willingness to trust. If we see Him as a harsh judge, we'll hide from Him. If we see Him as an indifferent force, we'll assume our lives have no value. But if we see Him as the Truth made flesh, Jesus, Who is both sovereign and loving, then His all-knowing nature doesn't erase our purpose, it anchors it.

What Is Truth?
In a world full of noise, opinions, and carefully crafted narratives, it's easy to feel disoriented. Social media shouts, influencers persuade, culture sways, and even religious circles can send mixed messages. The Truth can begin to feel like a moving target. Just when you think you've grabbed hold of it, it shifts.

But what if Truth isn't meant to be chased down like a runaway balloon?

What if Truth is calling out to you? What if Truth is chasing you?

Proverbs 8, gives us a stunning picture of what that looks like:
"Does not Wisdom call out? Does not understanding raise her voice? At the highest point along the way, where the paths meet, she takes her stand. 'To you, O people, I call out; I raise my voice to all mankind'" (Proverbs 8:1–4, NIV).

Wisdom: God's Wisdom isn't hiding. She's calling. Truth doesn't sit silently, waiting for the qualified or the elite to find it. Truth *pursues*. And just like Wisdom in Proverbs 8, Truth raises His voice in the middle of chaos, confusion, and crossroads.

But what if Truth isn't meant to be chased down like a runaway balloon?

So, if you've ever felt lost, unsure, or afraid to trust, you're not alone. The Bible often describes humanity as "sheep without a shepherd." That phrase might sound outdated, but it's deeply relevant today. Sheep are vulnerable without a guide. They wander, they get hurt, and they follow the wrong voices. And that's what happens to us spiritually when we don't know who to trust or what to believe.

But here's the good news: God doesn't leave Truthseekers in confusion. He speaks. He guides. He leads.

Truth doesn't change with public opinion. Truth has a voice. And He's calling *you*.

Faith vs. Doubt: When Reality Feels Blurry

Sometimes, even when we hear Truth calling, something inside of us hesitates. We want clarity, but we also crave control. We want faith, but we'd rather have certainty. That's the internal war between trust and understanding, surrender and self-reliance.

> *"Now faith is the substance of things hoped for, the evidence of things not seen"* (Hebrews 11:1, NKJV).

Faith requires us to move before everything is visible. It asks us to anchor our lives in something deeper than circumstances, opinions, or feelings. But for the Truthseeker, this can feel impossible, especially if your soul has been tossed by disappointment, deception, or trauma.

That's why the Garden of Eden still speaks.

There, we see two trees: The Tree of Life and The Tree of the Knowledge of Good and Evil.

One tree offered intimacy with God and access to His Wisdom, the Truth that brings life.

The other offered independence, control, and the illusion of enlightenment. But instead of Wisdom, it brought death and disconnection.

In today's culture, we still reach for the wrong tree. We're surrounded by voices offering knowledge, empowerment, and truth "on our own terms." But it's deception dressed up in freedom. It promises clarity, but delivers confusion. It encourages self-trust, but quietly severs the soul from the only Source of life.

We are made to be personally sourced by God. Truth isn't just a set of ideas. Truth is, a person who personally sources His people.

Jesus said,
> "I am the way, the Truth, and the life. No one comes to the Father except through Me" (John 14:6, NKJV).

And in John 8:32, He promised:
> "You shall know the truth, and the truth shall make you free" (NKJV).

The word truth in that verse is the Greek Word alētheia, meaning "what is real," "what is unconcealed," and "what cannot be hidden or falsified."

Truth, then, is not subjective. It is not a feeling. It's not based on how we were raised or how persuasive the latest podcast sounds.

Truth is God's reality revealed, trustworthy, and freeing.

When you choose faith in Jesus, you choose the Tree of Life. You reject confusion for clarity, lies for reality, and control for surrender. You turn toward the Shepherd and let Him lead.

Truth is God's reality revealed, trustworthy, and freeing.

What Is Truth? The Call of Wisdom

> *"Can't you hear the voice of Wisdom? From the top of the mountain of influence, she speaks into the gateways of the glorious city. At the place where pathways merge, at the entrance of every portal, there she stands ready to impart understanding, shouting aloud to all who enter ..."* (Proverbs 8:1–2, TPT).

Wisdom isn't hiding. Truth isn't avoiding you. He's calling out clearly, directly, and unwaveringly.

Proverbs, chapter 8, paints a vivid picture: Wisdom isn't speaking in code; she's crying out in the open, at the gates, in the public square, at every crossroads. In other words, at the very places where decisions are made and paths are chosen, Truth offers Himself.

Truth is not a philosophical theory or a poetic ideal. It's the spiritual reality that many overlook while searching in all the wrong places. Truth is *revealed*, not invented. We can't even "figure" God out. God is self-revealing. Revelation is a gift, not something we construct with personal preference or cultural consensus.

> *"All my words are clear and straightforward to everyone who possesses spiritual understanding. If you have an open mind, you will receive revelation knowledge"* (Proverbs 8:9, TPT).

Wisdom, personified, is not whispering in the dark. She cries out in compassion, reaching for anyone with ears to hear.

Sheep Without a Shepherd

Truthseekers are like sheep, curious, hungry, and prone to wander. They don't set out to get lost. They drift slowly pulled by other voices, comforts, and the lure of control, and soon find themselves exposed and vulnerable, surrounded by wolves of deception and spiritual confusion. They wander away from the Shepherd but later find out there are dangerous wolves ready to devour them, so they run back to their shepherd for protection.

God's response to the wandering is not condemnation. It's compassion. He said to me one day:

"Compassion is your story. You lead not because you are an expert but because you have seen My Face and My desire for My people. To shepherd them to Me. You scare the wolves. As your Shepherd, I want you to know I will not lead you astray, when you have been seeking me in humility and in the sincerity of your heart. My love will always lead you to my Truth."

There's a quiet authority in compassion. It draws pain close in order to heal. And when you live as someone led by the Shepherd, your very presence rooted in Truth becomes a warning to the enemy: These sheep are not unguarded.

The Two Trees

To understand the spiritual war over the Truth, we must go back to the beginning. Eden.

There, in the garden of perfection, were two trees. One was the Tree of Life, offering nourishment of God's presence, the substance of divine wisdom, and the revealed Truth; both Logos (the eternal Word) and Rhema (the spoken and revealed Word in action).

The other tree, the Tree of Knowledge of Good and Evil, seemed enlightening: facts, data, moral reasoning, and control. It offered what "made sense" but led to death. That was why God told man from the beginning not to eat of that tree.

The Tree of Life is rooted in revelation.

This is why Jesus is revealed to us as the Logos in John 1:1; He is the divine logic, the order, the meaning behind all creation. In Him, the Word is not merely an abstract principle but a living Person. As Graphe (the written Scriptures), the written Word finds its coherence and authority in Him. He is the mind of God revealed in words that endure. Yet, Jesus does not remain confined to the page; everything He speaks is Rhema embodied: life-giving, active, piercing, and creative (Hebrews 4:12). His words are not merely sound, but Spirit and life (John 6:63).

Therefore, when we feed on the Tree of Life, Christ Himself, we are not just gathering information, but receiving revelation, wisdom, and freedom. The enemy tempts us to substitute control, facts, and self-sufficient reasoning in place of divine revelation, but only in Christ as Logos, Graphe, and Rhema do we encounter the Truth that sets us free. (John 8:32).

The Tree of the Knowledge of good and evil is rooted in self-determination.

One gives life. The other poisons it.

Today, the same two trees still speak. We scroll, read, debate, and choose over and over again. But what tree are we feeding on?

Faith trusts the unseen. It leans into mystery and receives Truth as a person, not an argument.

> *"Faith is the substance of things hoped for, the evidence of things not seen"* (Hebrews 11:1, NKJV).

But knowledge disconnected from God can become deception. It sounds right, appears logical, and substantiates itself with data and evidence, yet it subtly erodes hope and distances the soul from the Truth that sets it free.

> *"Jesus said, 'And You shall know the truth, and the truth shall make you free'"* (John 8:32, NKJV).

When we believe in a lie about ourselves, God, and the world, we become subject to that lie's authority. In that area, we lose freedom. But when God reveals Truth to our hearts, we're released, restored, and realigned.

A Personal Challenge to the Truthseeker

God never created you to chase shadows or survive on partial light. You were made for *alētheia* truth in its fullest, rawest, most liberating form. That means reality as God defines it, not as culture bends it.

Follow the Shepherd. If you've wandered, run back. Not with shame, but with trust. He's not angry; He's waiting. And the wolves won't follow where He leads.

You may feel lost, uncertain, or overwhelmed. But you are not abandoned. You are being called by name into what is real.

A Prayer for the One Who Feels Confused

Father of Truth,

I confess sometimes it feels like I don't know what to believe. There are so many voices, so many opinions, and so many doubts trying to steal my peace. But I believe You are not hiding. I believe You are calling me through the noise, through my fear, and even through my questions.

Speak clearly, Lord. Let Wisdom rise louder than confusion. Help me to trust You when things don't make sense. Give me the discernment to reject the false and the courage to follow the Truth even when it costs me.

Shepherd of my soul, lead me back to the Tree of Life. Teach me to hunger for revelation, not just information. And where I've believed a lie, show me. I want to walk in Truth that sets me free. Amen

Journal Prompt

Examine the trees. Ask yourself: What am I feeding on? Am I drawing strength from the Tree of Life, God's revealed Word and presence? Or have I been nibbling on the Tree of Knowledge, relying on facts, feelings, or philosophies that make sense but don't bring peace?

_____
_____
_____
_____
_____
_____
_____

Listen for Wisdom. She is still crying out in the middle of your confusion, your doubt, your fatigue. Stop and lean in. Read Proverbs 8 out loud. Ask God to make her voice louder than every lie you've believed.

_____
_____
_____
_____
_____
_____
_____

Scripture Reflection

"The Lord God took the man and put him in the garden of Eden to work it and keep it. And the Lord God commanded the man, saying, 'You may surely eat of every tree of the garden, but of the tree of the knowledge of good and evil you shall not eat, for in the day that you eat of it you shall surely die'" (Genesis 2:15-17, ESV).

Chapter 3

The Truth That Stands Alone

Dear Truthseeker,

I had a deeply revealing conversation with my daughter one evening. We were talking about abortion not to debate, but to explore how truth is perceived when hard decisions must be made. It reminded me of a governor in ancient Rome called Pontious Pilate, I found it very ironic that when he encountered Jesus and, in his pursuit, to find the truth he asked Jesus; Truth Himself "What is truth?" (John 18:38). In that moment, Truth was standing right in front of him, yet he could not perceive Him.

Truth is not an opinion. It's not a position, a policy, or even a principle. Truth is a Person. And His name is Jesus.

When it comes to topics like abortion, the culture will use words like "pro-choice" to cloak deeper realities. But long before any government gave a woman the right to choose, God had already given humanity the power of choice. In Deuteronomy 30:19, God says,
> *"I have set before you life and death, blessing and cursing: therefore, choose life, that both you and your seed may live"* (NKJV).

Truth is not an opinion. It's not a position, a policy, or even a principle. Truth is a Person. And His name is Jesus.

The love of God is rooted in choice. John 3:16 says,
"For God so loved the world that He gave His only
begotten Son, that whoever believes in Him shall
not perish but have everlasting life" (NKJV).

That word "believes" is an invitation to choose; to choose *the*
Truth that stands alone.

When we recognize that truth is not relative, but absolute,
rooted in the character and person of Jesus, we begin to
understand the urgency and power behind the choices we make
every day. The choice to follow Jesus is not simply a religious
ritual or moral checklist. It's a life-altering decision to align
with reality itself, the source of all meaning and purpose.

Truth isn't something we create or adjust; it's something we
discover, receive, and live by. It's not just trying harder. It's not
more religious effort. It's truth and not just any truth, but *the*
Truth.

Why Truth Is Not Relative
In today's culture, you've probably heard people say, "That's
your truth, but not mine," or "truth is whatever you believe it to
be." It sounds fair and kind, but when you really stop to think
about it, that idea doesn't hold up, especially when it comes to
the biggest questions of life: Who am I? Why am I here? What
happens after I die?

The Bible tells us that truth is not some flexible idea shaped by
opinions or circumstances. Our perception of truth shifts upon
discovery and revelation. Truth is rooted in the very nature of
God; unchanging, eternal, and absolute. In John 14:6, Jesus
says something bold and unmistakable:
"I am the way, the truth, and the life. No one comes
to the Father except through me" (NKJV*)*.

Notice He doesn't say, "I am one way," or "I am one truth among many." He claims to be the Truth Himself, the ultimate reality.

Truth is absolute because it is God Himself, Who is unchanging and eternal.

If truth were relative, then Jesus' claim would be just one opinion among many, and salvation would be uncertain. But because God is constant and faithful, His truth stands firm across time and culture. In realizing this "our truth" shifts.

This is why we can trust God's Word and the person of Jesus Christ to be our anchor. When everything around us shifts, what we seek in Him remains steady.

Isaiah 40:8 states,
> *"The grass withers, the flower fades, but the word of our God will stand forever"* (NKJV).

Our identity, our hope, and our purpose are all found in this secure truth, not in what changes from one moment to the next.

Truth isn't something we create or adjust; it's something we discover, receive, and live by.

Why does this matter? Because if truth were just relative, then every belief would be equally valid, and nothing would have real meaning or power. How could we trust Jesus' promise of salvation if it were just one opinion among many? How could we find real peace or purpose if truth shifted like the wind?

The Bible reminds us that God's truth stands firm forever: "The grass withers, the flower fades, but the word of our God will stand forever" (Isaiah 40:8).

The Bible reminds us that God's truth stands firm forever: "The grass withers, the flower fades, but the word of our God will stand forever" (Isaiah 40:8). This means the foundation of our faith in Jesus Christ is rock solid.

This means the foundation of our faith in Jesus Christ is rock solid.

God's character, His promises, and His Word does not change based on what's popular or what we feel at the moment. They are eternal.

Psalm 119:160a declares, *"The entirety of Your word is truth,"* (NKJV), showing us that God's revelation to us through Scripture is trustworthy and complete. Our hearts and minds can rest in this truth because it reflects God's perfect and holy nature.

When we accept that truth is absolute and discover in Jesus, we are no longer tossed about by every new idea or cultural trend. We stand on firm ground in CHRIST. This truth frees us, guides us, and gives us hope even when life feels uncertain.

So, dear Truthseeker, the invitation is to lean into this unchanging truth, to let Him shape your life and your choices. It's not about bending truth to fit your desires; Allow Him, The Truth Himself, Jesus, to transform your heart and mind. Truth has leaned into you.

In a world that often says, "your truth, my truth," what do people mean? Perception, conviction, interpretation of reality. Are we good interpreters? It's easy to get lost in the idea that truth is relative, something that shifts with feelings, circumstances, or personal perspective. But the Bible shows us a different reality. It repeatedly shows us that God created us with the freedom to choose. This divine invitation highlights that choosing truth is fundamental to our very existence.

34

But with choice comes responsibility. Satan's deception in the Garden of Eden was a twisted attempt to usurp God's authority by convincing humanity that they could define good and evil for themselves. Yet, this "knowledge" without God's truth brought only confusion, fear, and death. This is why Christ remains our only secure interpreter of reality. Even now!

Jesus, on the other hand, as stated in the earlier chapter, offers us the Tree of Life, True life, and freedom through knowing Him. (John 10:10). Choosing Jesus means stepping into the light of truth, no longer slaves to lies or shifting standards.

So how do we walk in this truth daily? It begins with surrendering; letting go of the need to control or define truth for ourselves, and instead embracing Jesus as our guide, our truth, and our life. He is embracing you. It means allowing God's Word to shape our minds and our hearts and letting the Holy Spirit empower us to live in freedom and love.

Pilate's question still echoes today: *"What is truth?"* (John 18:38). What he failed to recognize is what many still fail to see today. Truth isn't just an idea to debate in courtrooms or classrooms; Truth is embodied in the person of Jesus Christ. Let's explore how this absolute truth is not just a concept, but a living reality that confronts and heals the broken places inside of us, setting us free from shame and lies.

Truth is not a floating principle; it is a Person. Again, Jesus didn't say He *knew* the truth. He said,
> *"I am the way, the truth, and the life. No one comes to the Father except through Me"* (John 14:6, NKJV)).

This singular claim dismantles the foundation of relative truth. If truth is a Person-unchanging, holy, and eternal, then truth cannot be whatever we feel in the moment. He cannot be molded by public opinion, cultural shifts, or emotional highs and lows. Truth stands when everything else falls.

This is the great offense of the gospel: its exclusivity. In a world that prides itself on inclusivity and personal autonomy, the gospel declares that there is only one way, one Name, and one Truth that leads to life. That can feel abrasive in a culture that values "your truth" and "my truth." But Truth, by nature, is exclusive; He defines reality and draws a clear line between what is and what is not.

The Paradox of Truth
When Jesus declared, "I am the way, the Truth, and the Life. No one comes to the Father except through Me" (John 14:6), He drew a line that many stumble over. His words are both radically exclusive and radically universal, a paradox that only makes sense when we see Truth as a Person, rather than a concept.

On the one hand, Jesus' claim is exclusive. He did not offer Himself as one option among many. He is not a guide pointing toward truth, but the very embodiment of it. Truth by its nature is exclusive; if something is true, then what contradicts it cannot be. When Jesus says He is the way, He shuts the door on every illusion that we can save ourselves or reach God by another path.

Yet at the very same time, His invitation is stunningly universal. The door is narrow, but it stands open to all. The gospel is not reserved for the elite, the powerful, or the religiously devout. It is for the broken, the weary, the searching, the sinner. John 3:16 proclaims that God's love extends to the entire world, every tribe, every nation, every heart willing to believe.

To our human minds, exclusivity and universality seem like opposites, but in Christ they converge. The paradox is resolved in Him:

- Exclusive in identity—Jesus alone is the Savior.
- Universal in scope—anyone can come to Him.

This is what makes the truth of Jesus unchanging. He is not subject to the shifting winds of culture, opinion, or preference. Hebrews 13:8 reminds us, "Jesus Christ is the same yesterday, today, and forever" (NKJV). His truth is both unyielding and inviting, a rock that cannot be moved, yet a door wide enough for the whole world to walk through.

Dear TruthSeeker, don't let the narrowness of the way discourage you, and don't let the wideness of the invitation confuse you. Instead, see the beauty of God's wisdom in this paradox: a love big enough to embrace the world, and a truth strong enough to remain unchanging.

Wisdom, personified, is not whispering in the dark. She is crying out in compassion, reaching for anyone with ears to hear.

Let's go back to Genesis for a moment. The serpent's strategy wasn't just to get Eve to eat the fruit, it was to distort God's truth. "Did God really say ...?" (Genesis 3:1). That one question introduced doubt, and where doubt enters, deception is quick to follow. Satan didn't need to turn Eve into a devil-worshipper; he just needed her to question the Word of God. That same question still tempts every Truthseeker today: *Did God really say?*

It's subtle, isn't it? We hear it in phrases like:
- "Well, that's just your interpretation."
- "God wouldn't want me to be unhappy."
- "Love is love."
- "My truth is valid." (It usually is, God attunes with our pain, and validates, freeing us from the lie.)

But truth that shifts to fit personal preference and questions God's voice is not truth at all. It's a shadow, a false image and a spiritual mirage that disappears when held up to the light of Christ.

Jesus came not only to save us from sin but to *reveal the truth* to expose every lie that holds us captive. Truth, when embraced, is not simply informational, it's transformational. It breaks chains. It heals shame and clarifies purpose.

The Apostle Paul wrote to the Ephesians:
"Then we will no longer be immature like children. We won't be tossed and blown about by every wind of new teaching ... Instead, we will speak the truth in love, growing in every way more and more like Christ" (Ephesians 4:14-15, NLT).

Truth and love are not opposites, they are companions. One without the other is either harsh or hollow. To walk in truth is to walk in Christ and to do so humbly, boldly, and lovingly in a world confused by counterfeits.

There's a quiet war raging all around you, one not fought with physical weapons, but with ideas, identities, and false definitions of love, freedom, and even God Himself. We don't always see it clearly, but we feel the effects of it: confusion, anxiety, self-doubt, spiritual numbness. The enemy's greatest tactic has always been deception. But Jesus, The Truth, has come to bring clarity, peace, and life.

When you surrender to Him, you're not just adopting a belief system. You're anchoring your soul to the One Who is reality. Not a version of it. Not a philosophy about it. But reality Himself.

When you surrender to Him, you're not just adopting a belief system. You're anchoring your soul to the One Who is reality. Not a version of it. Not a philosophy about it. But reality Himself.

This is why the Truth must stand alone. It needs no support, no validation, no cultural consensus. Jesus doesn't need to be voted in or explained away. He simply is. And when you meet Him, when you truly *know* Him, when you allow Him to know you, you're no longer swayed by every new trend, every new fear, or every new lie.

Truth steadies you.

Truth frees you.

Truth saves you.

This is the truth you were made to know, and He is not distant. The Truth that knows you. He is near. Knock, and the door will be opened. Seek, and you *will* find. (Matthew 7:7). (The door He's knocking on is inside of you.)

Personal Challenge to the Truthseeker
This week, pay attention to the voices shaping your view of truth. What sources influence your decisions; social media,

culture, fear, past trauma, or the Word of God? Write down one area of your life where you've wrestled with what's true. Then, intentionally seek God's Word on that topic. Let truth, not trend, be your guide. Ask the Holy Spirit to reveal any deception you've unknowingly believed.

A Prayer

Father of Truth,

I confess that I have, at times, chased lies that seemed easier than The Truth. But I no longer want to live by shadows and half-answers. Jesus, you are the Truth that stands alone. Root me in You. Let Your voice be louder than the noise of this world. I break every agreement I've made with deception; teach me how to walk in the light of what is real.
In Your name, I choose truth today. Amen.

Journal Prompt
Where have you felt most confused or uncertain lately? What would it look like to let Jesus, the Truth speak into that place? Write as if He were responding to you directly.

_____
_____
_____
_____
_____
_____
_____
_____
_____
_____
_____

Scripture Reflection
John 18:37-38,

"For this purpose, I was born and for this purpose I have come into the world to bear witness to the truth. Everyone who is of the truth listens to my voice" (ESV).

Pilate said to him, "What is truth?" Note that in that passage, Jesus was silent. What does the silence speak to you?

_____

_____

_____

_____

_____

_____

_____

_____

Reflect: In a world still echoing Pilate's question, will you be someone who listens to Jesus' voice?

_____

_____

_____

_____

_____

_____

_____

_____

"Prize wisdom highly and exalt her, and she will exalt and promote you. She will bring you to honor when you embrace her" (Proverbs 4:8, AMPC).

Chapter 4

A Hope You Can't Manufacture

Dear Truthseeker,

Are you running in circles, does it feel like you are always chasing after something, yet never able to catch up? You never quite feel settled. No matter how much you do, something always feels off? Like hope is just out of reach? What if that restlessness isn't meant to be your permanent state? What if your struggle to fix things yourself is a signal not of failure but of misplaced hope?

What if what you've been chasing was never meant to be manufactured at all? What if true hope, the kind that anchors your soul and brings deep rest was something you were created to receive, not fabricate?

The illusion of hope is just as dangerous as the absence of it. In a world saturated with filtered realities, surface-level belonging, and motivational mantras, it's no wonder we find ourselves chasing peace, identity, and meaning, yet never quite catching it. Like trying to hold water in our hands, this kind of hope leaks through the cracks of fear, doubt, performance, and exhaustion.

The Illusion of Community
We live in a time where the word "community" is everywhere, yet genuine connection feels rare. Social media makes it easy to express our deepest thoughts behind a screen, but when truth hides in the dark, it loses its power to transform. We've settled

for a version of belonging that requires no vulnerability and offers no healing. It's a community of shadows, not light.

Belonging is a word that's been passed around so often in our culture that it's lost both its weight and its worth. We talk about "community" while hiding behind screens. We celebrate "authenticity" while curating the version of ourselves we think will be accepted.

True belonging requires the courage to be seen and the safety to be known. That only happens in the presence of Truth. It's in authentic relationships, rooted in grace and accountability, that transformation takes place.

The Law of Boundaries (ref. boundaries.me by Henry Cloud)

The illusion of connection often comes from a lack of boundaries. We let people, opinions, and situations define us until we're stretched thin and lose ourselves in the process. But boundaries are a gift from God. Just like property lines tell you where your responsibility begins and ends, emotional and spiritual boundaries help you discern what is yours to carry and what is not.

True belonging requires the courage to be seen and the safety to be known. That only happens in the presence of Truth. It's in authentic relationships, rooted in grace and accountability, that transformation takes place.

To thrive and belong in community means you must abide by the laws of healthy boundaries. A person without boundaries is like a city with broken-down walls that are wide open to attack, vulnerable to deception, and overrun with the opinions and expectations of others.

44

"A person without self-control is like a city with broken-down walls" (Proverbs 25:28, NLT).

These are your boundaries:
- Your feelings
- Your thoughts
- Your attitudes and beliefs
- Your desires
- Your choices and behaviors
- Your values
- Your love, trust, and purpose

When you begin to recognize and reinforce these boundaries, you stop living in reaction to everything around you and start living from the Truth, Christ Himself within you. This is how you anchor your soul to authentically be able to hope again.

The Cost of Peace
Boundaries protect your peace. They are not walls to shut people out, but gates that guard what is sacred.

"A peaceful heart gives life to a healthy body" (Proverbs 14:30, NLT).

One of the most important truths you will ever learn on this journey is that *peace is not optional.* Jesus, the Truth is the Prince of Peace. He said in John 14:27,
*"**Peace I** leave with **you**; my **peace I give** to **you**. Not as the world **gives** do **I give** to **you**. Let not **your** hearts be troubled, neither let them be afraid" (NKJV).*

Peace is a vital force that strengthens your resilience. It's not the absence of trouble, it's the presence of God. And anything that steals your peace is too expensive to keep.

Christmas season is my favorite time of year, but I realized how often I let negative thoughts and unresolved emotions rob me of the joy I long for. By talking to God, I learn to surrender those thoughts to Him, exchange them for His truth, and invite His peace to govern my heart in the season.

What about you, Truthseeker? What's stealing your peace and breaching your boundary? And are you willing to let it go?

The Path to Purpose

> *"Trust in the LORD with all your heart; do not depend on your own understanding. Seek his will in all you do, and he will show you which path to take"* (Proverbs 3:5-6, NLT).

God doesn't ask us to figure everything out; (the tree of the knowledge of good and evil); He asks us to trust Him. (the Tree of Life). And when we do, He leads us toward purpose, one step at a time. Not a manufactured, hustle-based version of purpose, but the kind that flows from who we are and whose we are.

You don't have to strive for a hope you were never meant to create. Let go of the illusion. Embrace the Truth. Walk the path He lays before you.

Real Hope Begins with Trust

When you base your hope on what you can do, earn, or control, it will always fail you. Manufactured hope eventually crumbles under the weight of reality. But biblical hope is rooted in someone outside of you—Truth Himself. We trust in what He did, does, and is doing. Can you see it?

God's vision brings clarity, direction, and peace. It moves you from striving to resting, from surviving to trusting. You are not just an accident or a body trying to stay alive.

You are a marvel of divine engineering, designed with purpose, made with intention, and called to live in hope.

You were never meant to live aimlessly. Your very existence reflects divine design. Just consider this:
Your heart pumps 8,000 gallons of blood every day ... your veins stretch 100,000 miles ... your DNA, if unraveled, could reach to the sun and back 600 times.

You weren't made randomly. You were made intentionally.

You are a marvel of divine engineering, designed with purpose, made with intention, and called to live in hope.

The Need for Vision
Without vision, we flounder. Vision and community are related because we see ourselves in God and others' reflection, and we see Him to see our own self.
Without purpose, we drift. But when we receive and embrace God's vision for our lives, we find clarity, focus, and joy.

Truth, by its nature, cannot flourish in hiding. Truth must be expressed in the light, in places where we are known and still loved, seen and still safe. That kind of community, the kind that reflects heaven, isn't built on shared interests or self-protective alliances. It's built on spiritual wisdom and the courage to show up naked and unashamed.

Wisdom exposes the illusion, but it also extends the invitation: Come out of hiding. Step into the light. Belong again not to a false version of community, but to the God Who sees you.

"Where there is no vision from God, the people run wild, but those who adhere to God's instruction know genuine happiness!" (Proverbs 29:18, VOICE).

Personal Challenge to the Truthseeker

Where have you placed your hope? Is it in your job or in your ability to control outcomes? A relationship? Your own efforts to fix what's broken? Identify one area where you've been striving in your own strength. This week, surrender it. Not just mentally, but actively. Lay it before God. Then ask Him, *"What is Your truth in this area, and how do You want me to rest in it?"* Trust is receptive, but not passive; it's the most courageous act of hope you can take.

A Prayer for Hope and Rest

Father,

I confess that I've been running on empty, trying to manufacture peace, joy, and hope on my own. But You didn't create me to live that way. You created me to rest in You, to trust in Your Word, and to walk in the freedom of truth. Today, I surrender my striving. I give You every burden I've carried and every outcome I've tried to control. Help me to trust that You are enough. Fill my heart with Your peace, show me how You see me through Your eyes. Let my hope be built not on what I can do, but on Who You are. In Jesus' name, Amen.

Journal Prompt

What does "peace" look like for you right now?
Where do you feel most unsettled, and what truth from God's
Word do you need to anchor you in that area? Imagine Truth
standing before you. What does He say? What is He doing?

_____

_____

_____

_____

_____

_____

Scripture Reflection
Isaiah 26:3,
*"You will keep in perfect peace all who trust in you, all whose
thoughts are fixed on you"* (NLT).

When your mind is fixed on Him, peace isn't just possible, it's
promised.

Psalm 139, (NLT)
"O Lord, you have examined my heart, and know everything
    about me.
You know when I sit down or stand up. You know my thoughts
    even when I'm far away.
You see me when I travel, and when I rest at home.
You know everything I do. You know what I am going to
    say even before I say it, Lord.
You go before me and follow me. You place your hand of
    blessing on my head.
Such knowledge is too wonderful for me, too great for me to
    understand!
I can never escape from your Spirit! I can never get away from
    your presence!

If I go up to heaven, you are there; if I go down to the grave, you are there.

If I ride the wings of the morning, if I dwell by the farthest oceans, even there your hand will guide me, and your strength will support me.

I could ask the darkness to hide me, and the light around me to become night— but even in darkness I cannot hide from you. To you the night shines as bright as day.

Darkness and light are the same to you.

You made all the delicate, inner parts of my body, and knit me together in my mother's womb.

Thank you for making me so wonderfully complex! Your workmanship is marvelous—how well I know it.

You watched me as I was being formed in utter seclusion, as I was woven together in the dark of the womb.

You saw me before I was born.

Every day of my life was recorded in your book.

Every moment was laid out before a single day had passed.

How precious are your thoughts about me, O God. They cannot be numbered!

I can't even count them; they outnumber the grains of sand.

And when I wake up, you are still with me!

O God, if only you would destroy the wicked!

Get out of my life, you murderers!

They blaspheme you; your enemies misuse your name.

O Lord, shouldn't I hate those who hate you?

Shouldn't I despise those who oppose you?

Yes, I hate them with total hatred, for your enemies are my enemies.

Search me, O God, and know my heart; test me and know my anxious thoughts.

Point out anything in me that offends you, and lead me along the path of everlasting life" (NLT).

Chapter 5

The Way, The Truth, and The Life

Dear Truthseeker,

Have you ever received a gift only to discover it was already yours? It can leave you feeling confused or even deceived. That's how I felt when I realized just how much of my identity, in Christ, I had forfeited by believing lies. Not just lies about my worth, but lies about Who God is and how He works.

You Shall Be Like God?
There's an ancient lie that still echoes in our hearts today.

> *"'You will not certainly die,' the serpent said to the woman. 'For God knows that when you eat from it your eyes will be opened, and you will be like God ...'"* (Genesis 3:4–5, NIV).

The irony? Adam and Eve were already like God. They had been made in His image. But Satan twisted the truth just enough to plant a seed of doubt, and the moment they acted on it, everything changed.

The same deception still works today. "You're missing out." "God's holding something back." "If you just do this, you'll finally be in control." The enemy promises empowerment, but delivers bondage. He offers knowledge, but steals intimacy. He promises freedom, but leads to shame. What if the empowerment and freedom are already yours?

It's one thing to know about Jesus. It's another thing to understand and experience: He is the Way, Truth, and Life. This isn't just a poetic line; it's a radical declaration of exclusivity and a revolutionary invitation to restoration.

> *"Jesus answered, 'I am the way and the truth and the life. No one comes to the Father except through me'"* (John 14:6, NIV).

This single verse in the Bible unravels every man-made path to peace and truth. Jesus didn't say He *knew* the way. He didn't say He *taught* the truth. He said, **"I AM."** That "I AM" points us back to Exodus 3:14 where God revealed His name to Moses: *"I AM WHO I AM."* Jesus is not a way among many, He is the **only** way back to the Father, because He is the embodiment of the Truth we're all seeking and the Life we were always meant to live.

> *"I will ascend above the tops of the clouds; I will make myself like the Most High"* (Isaiah 14:14, NIV).

This wasn't just Satan's lie, it was his *ambition*. His rebellion in heaven became his mission on earth. If he couldn't be like God, he'd convince God's image-bearers to hand over their dominion. And we did. Through sin, we lost the inheritance that had been ours all along.

But Jesus, the Way, the Truth, and the Life stepped in. He came not just to expose the lie, but to **redeem what was lost**. He came to restore your inheritance and reclaim the authority that was surrendered in Eden.

The Battle for Your Inheritance
This is more than theology. It's spiritual warfare.

Satan isn't fighting for your attention; he's after your inheritance. He doesn't want you walking in truth, because truth leads to freedom. He doesn't want you walking in purpose, because purpose glorifies God. He wants you stuck in cycles of shame, performance, comparison, and confusion. Because as long as you're uncertain about *who you are*, you'll never fully walk in what's already been given to you.

But Truth exposes the lie. Truth restores the broken. Truth invites us to choose a different path—not one of striving, but of surrender.

You don't have to create your own truth. You are an image bearer. You were made to walk in the Truth Who came to rescue you.

You don't have to create your own truth. You are an image bearer. You were made to walk in the Truth Who came to rescue you.

Living in the Truth That Redeems
Truth isn't just a concept. It's a Person. And once you've encountered Him, you can't unknow Him.

To follow Jesus the Way, the Truth, and the Life requires a surrender of your version of truth. It requires dying to a false self, so that you might truly live. It's not always easy, but it is always worth it. He doesn't just lead you to life. He is your life.

And yet, even after we believe in Jesus as The Truth, there's still a choice to be made: **Will you live like you've been redeemed? Or will you keep living as if the lie still holds power?**

Jesus didn't come to make your life a little better. He came to raise the dead. He came to **undo the curse**, reclaim your purpose, and restore your access back to the Father.

And because of that, you can surrender striving to be like God.

You already belong to Him and bear His image.

Personal Challenge to the Truthseeker
What lie have you been living under? Identify one area in your life where the enemy has whispered, "You're not enough," "You've missed it," or "You need to fix this yourself." Then, replace that lie with the truth of God's Word. Write it down. Speak it aloud. And declare: "I choose Truth."

You've already been given an inheritance. Now walk in it.

A Prayer of Surrender to the Truth

Father,

Thank You for sending Jesus, the Way, the Truth, and the Life to rescue me. I confess that I have listened to lies and tried to fix things in my own strength. But I choose now to believe the Truth. I surrender the areas I've tried to control, and I trust You with my identity, my future, and my freedom. Redeem what's been lost. Restore what's been stolen. Reclaim every part of me for Your glory. I belong to You. In Jesus' name, Amen.

Journal Prompt

Where in your life have you felt the need to "be like God" to control, to know everything, or to fix what's broken on your own?

_____
_____
_____
_____
_____
_____
_____
_____

What would it look like to surrender that area to Jesus, the Truth?

_____
_____
_____
_____
_____
_____
_____
_____

Scripture Reflection
Colossians 1:13–14,
"He has delivered us from the domain of darkness and transferred us to the kingdom of his beloved Son, in whom we have redemption, the forgiveness of sins" (ESV).

You have been delivered. You have been transferred. You are redeemed. Walk in that truth today.

Chapter 6

Religion vs. Relationship

Dear Truthseeker,

There's a kind of tired that sleep can't fix, a soul-weariness that creeps in when we're trying to do all the right things but still feel like we're missing something. We check the boxes; we say the prayers; and we do our best to be good, but still feel distant from the One we're trying to please.

That's the trap of religion.

For years, I thought I had to get everything just right to be loved by God. If I prayed enough, served enough, repented enough then *maybe* I would be accepted. Maybe I'd be blessed. Maybe I'd finally have peace.

But religion without relationship is exhausting. It reduces faith to performance and God to a supervisor. And the more I strived, the less I felt known.

One morning, in a moment of quiet desperation, I turned to Psalm 143:8. It felt like the cry of my own heart:
> *"Cause me to hear Your loving-kindness in the morning, for on You do I lean and in You do I trust. Cause me to know the way wherein I should walk, for I lift my inner self to You."*

This verse stopped me in my tracks. It wasn't about striving. It was about leaning in. Not about proving but trusting. It was a reminder that God isn't looking for performance, He's looking for surrender. He wants my *inner self*, not my outward display.

The Trap of Religion

Religion without relationship is an easy counterfeit to fall into. It appeals to our human desire for structure, rules, and measurable progress. But underneath the surface, it can become a dangerous cycle of shame and striving.

Religion says:
> "Perform better."
> "Clean yourself up first."
> "God is watching; don't mess up."

But Jesus never invited us into a performance-based faith. He called us into **fellowship**; a relationship rooted in grace, not guilt.

Throughout the gospels, Jesus often clashed with the Pharisees, not because they were religious, but because their hearts were far from God. They knew the law, but missed the love. They had information, but no intimacy.

> *"These people honor Me with their lips, but their hearts are far from Me"* (Matthew 15:8, NKJV).

The trap of religion is that it can look holy on the outside, but be completely empty on the inside. Jesus didn't come to improve our religious systems. He came to fulfill them and to tear down every wall that keeps us from knowing God personally.

He didn't die so you could follow a set of rules. He died so you could be in relationship.

And that's the invitation; to step out of the exhausting cycle of trying to earn what has already been given, and into the rest of simply being with the One Who loves you.

He didn't die so you could follow a set of rules. He died so you could be in relationship.

Jesus and the Religious Elite

Jesus wasn't crucified for healing people or preaching love. He was crucified because He disrupted the very foundation of the religious establishment.

To the Pharisees and Sadducees, righteousness was measured in rule-following, in public displays of holiness, and in maintaining a distance from the "unclean." But Jesus turned all of that upside down. He touched the leper, He sat with sinners, He forgave the adulterer, and He healed on the Sabbath.

He didn't just challenge their theology; He exposed their hearts.

> *"Woe to you, teachers of the law and Pharisees, you hypocrites! You are like whitewashed tombs, which look beautiful on the outside but on the inside are full of the bones of the dead ..."* (Matthew 23:27, NKJV).

Jesus' harshest words were not to the broken, but to the proud. He wasn't repelled by sin; He was repelled by spiritual arrogance masquerading as holiness.

The religious elite were convinced they were close to God because of their traditions. But Jesus, the Truth, showed that proximity to ritual means nothing without proximity to Him.

And that leads us to the invitation ...

The Invitation to Intimacy
In a world obsessed with achievement, it's hard to accept that you don't have to earn God's love.

The truth is: **you already have it.**

"But God demonstrates His own love for us in this: While we were still sinners, Christ died for us" (Romans 5:8, NKJV).

That means you don't have to "get it all together" to come close. You don't have to clean yourself up before stepping into His presence. In fact, the only way to truly be clean is to **come close**.

He isn't calling you to religion.

He's calling you to relationship. To walk with Him. To hear His voice. To lift your inner self to Him like Psalm 143:8 says, and trust that He will show you the way to walk.

Religion will always demand more.

Jesus says, "Come to Me."

The Danger of Performance-Based Faith
Performance-based faith is subtle. It disguises itself as discipline, responsibility, even devotion. But the underlying message is toxic: *God loves me more when I do better.*

It creeps in through comparison:
"She prays more than I do."
"He knows the Bible better than I do."
"They must be closer to God."

It sneaks into our quiet time:
"If I miss a day, I've failed."
"If I don't feel anything, God must be disappointed."

It attaches shame to our spiritual rhythms and turns grace into guilt. But this was never the life Jesus called us to.

> *"Remain in Me, as I also remain in you. No branch can bear fruit by itself; it must remain in the vine"* (John 15:4, NKJV).

Abiding is not about striving, it's about **staying**.

In performance-based faith, you try to do everything for God. In relationship, you learn to do everything with Him.

It's not about being enough. It's about being **with** the One Who is already with you.

You were not designed to *earn* love. You were made to *receive* it. And when you do, everything else flows from that place, peace, obedience, joy, freedom.

In performance-based faith, you try to do everything for God. In relationship, you learn to do everything with Him.

Living in Freedom
The beauty of a relationship with Jesus is that it doesn't just free you *from* something, it frees you *for* something. You

are no longer bound to fear, shame, or spiritual performance. You are free to walk in peace. You are free to be loved without condition. You are free to be led by the Spirit, not driven by pressure.

> *"Now the Lord is the Spirit, and where the Spirit of the Lord is, there is freedom"* (2 Corinthians 3:17, NKJV).

Freedom isn't lawlessness. It's life in alignment with Love. It's walking with Jesus moment by moment, not trying to impress Him from afar. It's waking up with a heart that says, "Cause me to hear Your loving-kindness in the morning ... for I lift my inner self to You" (Psalm 143:8).

When you stop performing and start abiding, everything shifts. This is where legalism loses its grip.

This is where shame gives way to joy. Not because you did everything right, but because you've chosen to live in the freedom of being His.

This is where striving ends and intimacy begins.

Striving is when we attempt to prove ourselves worthy before God through performance, discipline, or outward religious acts. It often comes from a place of fear, insecurity, or the belief that God's love must be maintained by our effort. Striving is exhausting because it makes intimacy conditional, if we do well, we feel close to God; if we fail, we feel distant and ashamed.

Dear Truthseeker, this is where I was fifteen years ago. I was striving to maintain God's love through my own efforts. I had a marriage that was falling apart, and a three-year-old daughter

I was struggling to tend to on my own. Church was my outlet; my gifts to serve God's people were my way of intimacy with God. I was exhausted. Then one morning, lying on the cold floor in the prayer room of my church, I asked the Lord to take His gift of prophecy away because I was tired of hearing Him for others, but I couldn't hear His voice to fix my mess. Then I heard Him say to me, *"I just want you to get to know me."* (an impression in my heart, not an audible voice).

Jesus never called us to strive; He called us to abide.

> *"Abide in me, and I in you. As the branch cannot bear fruit of itself, unless it abides in the vine, neither can you, unless you abide in me"* (John 15:4, NKJV).

Abiding is about resting in His finished work on the cross and living from a posture of trust. It's not passive, but it's not forced either. Instead of hustling to earn His approval, we cultivate awareness of His presence. Abiding is letting His Spirit do in us what we cannot do in ourselves, producing fruit naturally, like a branch connected to the vine.

How to stop striving and learn to abide:
1. Shift from performance to presence. Stop asking, "Am I doing enough?" and start asking, "Am I with Him?"
2. Receive before you give. Instead of pushing yourself to serve, pray, or lead from emptiness, pause and let His love fill you first.
3. Trust His work over yours. Remember, intimacy isn't about holding on tighter to Him, it's about realizing He's holding on to you. (John 10:28).
4. Practice rhythms of rest. Silence, worship, and prayer aren't checklists; they're invitations to simply be with Him.

When striving ends, you stop running on the treadmill of performance and step into the embrace of a God Who delights in you, not because of what you do, but because of who you are in Him. That's where intimacy grows, and effort becomes overflow instead of obligation.

Freedom in Christ isn't the absence of boundaries; it's the presence of belonging.

It's the kind of freedom that whispers; *you're already loved before you lift a finger.*

It's the permission to breathe deeply, to stop running, to rest in the arms of a Savior Who doesn't need you to be perfect—just present.

This freedom is beautiful because it **restores dignity**.

It brings your soul back to life.

No more pretending.

No more earning.

No more fearing that you'll never be enough.

Freedom in Christ isn't the absence of boundaries; it's the presence of belonging.

Instead, you begin to experience the kind of peace religion could never offer: the peace of being fully known and still fully loved.

Jesus didn't set you free just to save you from hell. He set you free so you could walk with Him, unburdened. So, you could

wake up each morning and say with confidence:
"I am loved. I am His. And I don't have to perform for what's already mine."

This is the freedom of grace. Not just a one-time gift, but a daily invitation. An invitation to live unshackled. To live at rest. To live in joy.

Personal Challenge to the Truthseeker
This week, notice where you've been striving. Is it in your prayer life, relationships, or even your attempts to "feel spiritual?" Instead of pushing harder, pause. Sit in silence with God, even for five minutes a day, and simply invite Him to be with you. Don't try to produce just abide. Get quiet and become aware of God's ever presence.

A Prayer for Freedom and Intimacy

Father,

I confess I've been trying to earn what You've already given me. I've mistaken religious effort for true relationship, and I've carried burdens You never asked me to carry. But today, I lay them down. I return to Your feet. I lift my inner self to You, just as Psalm 143:8 says.

Cause me to hear Your loving-kindness in the morning. Show me the way I should walk. I want to walk with You not just work for You. Thank You for the freedom to be fully known and fully loved. In Jesus' name, Amen.

Journal Prompt

Where have I been trying to perform for God instead of receiving His love freely?

What would shift if I stopped striving and started abiding in relationship?

_____

_____

_____

_____

_____

_____

_____

_____

_____

_____

_____

_____

_____

Scripture Reflection
Galatians 5:1,
"So Christ has truly set us free. Now make sure that you stay free, and don't get tied up again in slavery to the law" (NLT).

You are free not to wander, but to walk with Him.

Stay free, Truthseeker. You were never meant to carry shame again.

Chapter 7

Truth That Confronts and Heals

Dear Truthseeker,

You've come this far not just because you're curious about truth but because you're hungry for healing. And here's what you need to know now:

Healing always begins with honesty.

Not the kind that's filtered, edited, or polished to make pain easier to swallow, but the kind of honesty that stands in the presence of God and says, *"Here I am. Even this part of me."*

Comfort without confrontation leaves the root of the wound untouched. Healing only comes when the truth enters the hidden places of our lives, the ones we'd rather keep buried. Because love that never tells you the truth isn't love at all, it's flattery. And flattery doesn't free; it traps.

Read Jesus' encounter with the Samaritan woman in the book of John, chapter 4. At first, she sought comfort: water that would quench her thirst and save her from daily trips to the well. But Jesus didn't stop at her surface need; He spoke directly to the deeper truth of her life. He told her, "Go, call your husband," knowing full well she had no husband. In that moment, the Truth confronted her shame, her broken relationships, and the cycle she was trapped in.

But notice how Jesus did it. He wasn't cruel. He wasn't condemning. He simply revealed what was hidden so she could finally be healed. He acknowledged her reality in love, and instead of running away, she stayed. Why? Because His confrontation carried no malice, only the kind of love that frees. His truth was not meant to embarrass her but to open the door to living water.

Her healing didn't start when He promised her water; it started when He told her the truth. That moment of confrontation became the turning point that led her to run back to her town, proclaiming, "Come, see a man who told me everything I ever did. Could this be the Messiah?" The very thing she once hid in shame became the testimony that spread the gospel.

True healing works the same way in us. Jesus meets us where we are, comforts us with His presence, but He loves us too much to leave us there. His truth will face the sin, the shame, the self-deception we cling to. And if we stay with Him in that moment, we'll see that His confrontation isn't rejection—it's restoration.

If you're going to be truly healed, Truth can't just comfort you—it has to confront you.

Because love that never tells you the truth isn't love. It usually starts with honest "fessing up" from us—to allow ourselves to be known.

And truth that doesn't lead you to healing isn't Jesus.

> *"Beloved, I pray that in every way you may succeed
> and prosper and be in good health [physically], just
> as [I know] your soul prospers"* (3 John 1:2, AMP).

God desires you to be whole—spirit, soul, and body. But your soul can't flourish if it's still guarding wounds, concealing lies, or performing to gain approval. The wounds might not be your fault. However, healing is your invitation. That's why Truth came.

I recall a moment when I saw a vision of myself kneeling before the Lord. All around me were jagged shards of glass, which I understood to represent the broken pieces of my heart, my story, and my past. I bent down and began gathering them, one by one. As I held them, uncertain of what to do next, I heard Him speak softly: "Will you bring them to Me?"

I laid the broken pieces at His feet, and what He did next took my breath away.

He started picking up each shard, fitting them together carefully and intentionally. Gradually, piece by piece, he created a stunning mosaic vase. Not despite the cracks, but because of them. He crafted something that reflected Him.

Then I heard Him whisper:
The most beautiful thing is when My children bring Me their brokenness so I can create a version of Who I am in them. I resist the proud, but I give grace to the humble. Your posture of acknowledging your brokenness is your humility. And I will make beauty out of it.

I thought I had brought everything. But then He said, "Get the little pieces ... let nothing be wasted."

And with tears in my eyes, I whispered, "Thank You, Lord ... You are worthy of it all."

This is the kind of healing only Truth can provide. The kind that confronts not to shame you but to make you whole. The kind that calls you closer, not when you've cleaned yourself up, but when you're still bleeding.

The Nature of Truth
Truth isn't neutral. It's not passive. And it's never abstract.

Truth is a Person; Jesus Christ and when He enters a room, He doesn't sit quietly in the corner. He **speaks**, He **reveals**, and He **heals**. But first, He confronts what is false.

That's what makes truth so uncomfortable for the flesh. We want comfort without correction, healing without surrender, wholeness without exposure. But Jesus, in His mercy, doesn't allow that. He doesn't just patch up the surface. He goes straight to the root.

> *"And you shall know the truth, and the truth shall make you free"* (John 8:32, NKJV).

The word "know" here is about intimacy, not intellect.

It's the kind of knowing that happens when you've been changed by what's real.

Truth reveals what we've hidden.

Truth challenges what we've accepted.

Truth calls out what we've justified.

Truth dismantles the lies we've made friends with.

And this is key; Truth doesn't do it to shame you. It does it to **free** you.

Jesus doesn't expose what's broken so He can condemn it. He exposes it so He can **heal it**.

He is the kind of Savior Who says, "Show Me where it hurts."

He is the kind of Truth Who sits with you in the rubble and refuses to leave until you walk out whole. So, if this chapter stirs things that feel raw, exposed, or tender don't run. That discomfort isn't a sign of danger. It's the nearness of the Great Physician.

He loves you too much to leave your wounds covered in religious bandages. He's not in the business of behavior modification. He's after your **transformation**. And the power of transformation isn't in the *pretending*; it's in the *process*.

> *"Behold, you desire truth in the innermost being, and in the hidden part [of my heart] You will make me know wisdom"* (Psalm 51:6, AMP).

This is where real change happens, not just on the outside, but in the secret places. The places where trauma lives. The places where lies take root. The places we don't talk about.

God does His best work **there**.

He doesn't expose you to embarrass you. He exposes you to **heal** you. He longs for you to open your heart to Him and allow yourself to be known.

He's not trying to shame you. He's inviting you into **freedom**.

Lies We've Believed

Each of us carries lies we didn't intend to believe. Some were whispered in childhood, others came wrapped in pain. And some were so loud, so constant, that they began to sound like the truth. Maybe you believed you had to earn love, or that your worth depended on your performance. Maybe you learned to hide your emotions because vulnerability felt dangerous. Maybe someone told you, with words or silence, that you were too much or not enough. And maybe, without realizing it, you built your identity around the very thing that broke you.

This is why the healing journey isn't just about feeling better; it's about seeing clearly. Because when you believe in a lie, you live as if it's true. And where there's deception, there's bondage.

> *"When he lies, he speaks his native language, for he is a liar and the father of lies"* (John 8:44, NIV).

The enemy of your soul doesn't need to destroy you completely; he only needs to convince you of something that isn't true. He knows that if you accept a lie, you'll start living from a false identity. And once your identity is compromised, your purpose becomes distorted.

But here's the hope: **the same way you believed the lie, you can believe the Truth.**

You can unlearn false stories. You can reject shame. You can take your thoughts captive and make them obedient to Christ. (2 Corinthians 10:5). You can exchange deception for truth because Jesus didn't just come to save you.

He came to **restore who you were always meant to be.**

Truth isn't just a doctrine, it's a mirror. It shows you what was broken *and* what can be healed. It shows you what you were never meant to carry and what Jesus already carried for you.

The Gentle Confrontation of Jesus
Jesus never exposed people to crush them; He exposed them to heal them. And while His words could cut, they always carried compassion. His Truth never stood alone; it came with eyes of fire and a heart full of mercy.

Look again at the woman at the well. (John 4). She came with a bucket to draw water, but Jesus came to draw her into truth. He gently peeled back her story.

> *"You've had five husbands ... and the man you're with now isn't your husband."*

That wasn't shame it was invitation.

Invitation to **stop hiding.**

Invitation to **worship in spirit and truth.**

Invitation to be known and still loved.

Or consider the rich young ruler. (Mark 10). He came seeking eternal life. He kept the commandments. He had a good resume. But Jesus looked at him, **loved** him, and said:
> *"One thing you lack ..."*

Jesus wasn't after his possessions; He was after his heart.

And then there was Peter. Bold, passionate, and impulsive. Peter declared he would never deny Jesus; yet, within hours, he did so three times. The same mouth that proclaimed love spoke words of betrayal. But when Jesus rose, He came back for Peter.

And with every "Do you love Me?" He restored what shame had tried to erase.

That's the kind of Truth Jesus is. Not a cold fact, but a living Word.

Not a condemning voice, but a healing presence.

Not a courtroom judge, but a Good Shepherd who lays down His life for the sheep.

When Jesus confronts, it's not to destroy; it's to deliver.

When He uncovers the wound, it's because He has already prepared the oil.

The Path to Healing
Healing isn't a lightning strike; it's often a slow walk. Not because God lacks power, but because He's committed to the process. And the process, dear Truthseeker, is where your soul is rebuilt.

Some wounds heal quickly, while others take months or years. But the road to healing is always paved with the same stones.

Truth. Grace. Surrender. Time.
Jesus walks with us patiently, never forcing what we're not yet ready to release, but always nudging and inviting us into deeper freedom.

"He heals the brokenhearted and binds up their wounds" (Psalm 147:3, NIV).

To "bind up" in Scripture wasn't just a casual wrapping. It meant to dress, protect, and continually attend to the wound until it healed completely.

That's what Jesus does. He keeps showing up, not just once at the altar, but every time you're ready to bring Him another piece of your pain. **Some of us were taught that healing means we forget what happened. But in the Kingdom, healing often means we remember differently. The sting is gone, but the wisdom remains.**

The scar stays, but now it tells a story not of defeat, but of *deliverance.*

> *"Even my suffering was good for me, for it taught me to pay attention to your decrees"* (Psalm 119:71, NLT).

Healing teaches us to lean not on our understanding, but on His faithfulness.

It makes us brave, soft, humble, and whole. And most of all, it makes room for **other people to heal, too.** Because when God heals you, He doesn't just restore your story, He **redeems** it for someone else's breakthrough.

Personal Challenge to the Truthseeker
This week, invite the Holy Spirit to show you any area of your life where you've believed a lie or protected a wound. Don't rush past what feels uncomfortable. Instead, ask Him to sit with you there, and begin the healing process. Bring the broken

pieces to His feet. Even the small ones. Let nothing be wasted. Remember, the greatest freedom comes not from hiding your pain, but from surrendering it.

Prayer

Father,

I thank You that You are not afraid of my brokenness. You see every hidden wound and still draw near. Today, I choose to bring You every piece especially the ones I've been afraid to touch. Forgive me for the lies I've believed and the masks I've worn. Teach me how to live in truth, not just as a concept, but as a Person; Jesus. Heal the places I've ignored. Restore the parts I've given up on. Shape my story into something that reflects Your love and freedom. In Jesus' name, Amen.

Journal Prompt
What are the lies I've believed about myself, God, or others that have shaped how I view the world?

_____

_____

_____

_____

_____

_____

_____

_____

_____

_____

_____

_____

_____

What would it look like to invite Truth into those places?

_____

_____

_____

_____

_____

_____

_____

What pieces am I still holding onto instead of surrendering?

_____

_____

_____

_____

_____

_____

_____

_____

Scripture Reflection
"Beloved, I pray that in every way you may succeed and prosper and be in good health [physically], just as [I know] your soul prospers" (3 John 1:2, AMP).

"You shall know the truth, and the truth shall make you free" (John 8:32, NKJV).

"He heals the brokenhearted and binds up their wounds" (Psalm 147:3, NIV).

Chapter 8

Hope in the Middle of the Mess When Everything Feels Like It's Falling Apart

Dear Truthseeker,

Every life has a moment when the ground seems to shift beneath you. The diagnosis arrives, the marriage strains, the job ends, the dream dies, and the questions multiply. You look around and wonder, how did I end up here?

It's messy. It's hard. And in those moments, hope can feel like a cruel joke, like a word reserved for people who aren't facing real pain. But that's exactly where the gospel shines the brightest.

God is not waiting for you to get your life together before He shows up. He steps into the mess. He always has. From the Garden to the manger to the cross, He has been a God Who enters broken places and brings redemption from the inside out.

> *"The Lord is close to the brokenhearted and saves those who are crushed in spirit"* (Psalm 34:18, NIV).

Hope doesn't come from understanding everything. It comes from trusting the One Who holds everything, even when nothing makes sense.

In the middle of your chaos, God is not confused.

In the middle of your storm, He is not asleep.

In the middle of your failure, He has not withdrawn His love.

He is Emmanuel: **God with us** not just in theory, but in the thick of real life.

Carriers of Compassion

When I was young, I used to cry a lot, especially when I saw others in pain. I didn't understand why I was like that and wished it weren't so. Especially when my oldest sister would make fun of me and call me "a crybaby." I remember being very ill with a deadly disease called cholera. My father had come home unexpectedly from work; that was a miracle, because I probably would have died from the disease, but I will save part of the story for another time. Well, as we arrived at the hospital, I realized I was among those who had the same disease I did, and we were all in critical condition like me. My eyes met a very frail man who was in pain and agony. I immediately started crying because I felt so sad for him. When my dad asked why I was crying, I hesitated and told him I felt sad for the man in pain. My dad shook his head and said, "You are in the same situation, my love, and yet you cry for him?"

In my moment of feeling like I was falling apart, the Lord said to me, in the same voice inside that gives me unexplainable peace, and then my eyes well up with tears.

"What if I told you that what feels like your greatest weakness is actually your greatest strength? You are a weapon in My hands, and the enemy fears you. That's why you feel so deeply. That sensitivity you've questioned, even resented, is not a flaw;

it's by design. I wired you with a deep sense of compassion—not the kind the world copies, but My compassion. A supernatural ability to feel what others carry, to walk into broken spaces and see pain that hasn't been spoken yet. You've mistaken this sensitivity as a burden, but it's truly a gift. Very few of my people have it. It's unique to the assignment I've given you: to bring healing to the hurting, walk through their pain, recognize it, and lead them to Me.

But hear this:
You are not meant to carry everything, only what I give you.

I'm teaching you to distinguish between the emotions I've asked you to process and those I've asked you to intercede over and release. Even the pain you feel from others toward you. It's part of the training. It teaches you empathy, sharpens your discernment, and shapes you into a safe place for those who've never had one. This isn't just about emotional sensitivity; it's about spiritual clarity. You're learning to walk in step with Me. And hope isn't just what you receive; it's what you carry for others."

This is what it means to have hope in the middle of the mess ...

You don't deny the pain. You walk through it, becoming a path of healing for someone else.

What is the Lord saying to you?

> *"Blessed be the God ... who comforts us in all our tribulation, that we may be able to comfort those who are in any trouble, with the comfort with which we ourselves are comforted by God"* (2 Corinthians 1:3-4, NKJV).

Hope Doesn't Bypass the Pain; It's Formed Through It
If anyone told you that following Jesus would exempt you from suffering, they gave you the wrong gospel. The truth is hope is not the absence of pain; it's what grows when pain meets presence.

> *"We also glory in our sufferings, because we know that suffering produces perseverance; perseverance, character; and character, hope. And hope does not put us to shame, because God's love has been poured out into our hearts through the Holy Spirit"* (Romans 5:3-5, NIV).

Did you catch that?

Hope isn't instant; it's produced.

It's not false optimism or just positive thinking. It's born from the struggle of moving forward when everything in you wants to give up. It's trusting God even without a backup plan.

It's believing He's good *even when it doesn't feel good.*

Perseverance teaches you to keep walking.

Character teaches you who you are when no one's watching. And hope ... hope anchors you when the waves are relentless.

This is why the mess doesn't disqualify you; it *qualifies* you. The very thing you think discredits your faith might be what deepens it most. You're not broken beyond repair.

You're not failing at faith. You're becoming ... resilient, refined, and rooted.

"For You, O God, have tested us; You have refined us as silver is refined" (Psalm 66:10, NKJV).

Hope formed in suffering doesn't shatter easily. It's not hollow and it's not naive. It's been through fire and *found God faithful.*

Your Mess Is Not the End of the Story
Your story doesn't end where the mess began. It doesn't end with the divorce, the diagnosis, failure, or the fallout. It doesn't end with the trauma, the addiction, or the chapter you never thought you'd survive.

Why? Because the Author is still writing.

And He writes in redemptive ink.

What the enemy meant to destroy you, God is weaving into something you never could've written on your own, a testimony.

"And we know that in all things God works for the good of those who love him, who have been called according to his purpose" (Romans 8:28, NIV).

But here's what no one tells you about that verse: The *good* may not look like what you expected.

Sometimes the good is *healing*, not fixing.

Sometimes it's *peace*, not answers.

Sometimes it's *depth*, not escape.

God's definition of restoration isn't to return your life to what it was.

It's to make something *better* something *eternal*.

You are not your worst day.

You are not your brokenness.

You are not your shame.

You are His.

And hope is the assurance that He will finish what He started even if the path is messy.

He is not done.

Personal Challenge to the Truthseeker
Take time this week to reflect on the "messy" chapters of your life. The ones you've tried to forget or fix in your own strength. Ask God to show you where He was in those moments. Invite Him to speak hope over what still feels unfinished. Write down one area where you're still waiting for restoration and surrender it again, trusting the Author to keep writing.

Prayer

Jesus,

You are my hope in the middle of the mess.

You never turn away from brokenness instead, You step into it with mercy and truth.

Today, I surrender the pieces I've tried to hold together. I release the need to understand, fix, or escape. Instead, I ask

You to redeem. Teach me to trust You in the middle, not just at the end. Anchor my soul in Your faithfulness. Let my story be a testimony of how You make beauty from ashes and light from the darkest nights. In Your name I pray, Amen.

Journal Prompt
• Where in your life are you still waiting for healing or clarity?

_____
_____
_____
_____
_____
_____
_____
_____
_____
_____

• What does it mean for you to trust God *in the middle*, before the resolution comes?

_____
_____
_____
_____
_____
_____
_____
_____
_____
_____

• What does hope look like when it's no longer based on outcomes, but on God's presence?

_____
_____
_____
_____
_____
_____
_____
_____

• Do you have a testimony of how God gave you Hope in the middle of a mess? Write it down. Even if you are still in your mess, use this opportunity as a process to allow the Lord to speak to you in the middle of the mess right now. Ask Him what He is doing now.

_____
_____
_____
_____
_____
_____
_____
_____

Scripture Reflection

"We have this hope as an anchor for the soul, firm and secure" (Hebrews 6:19, NIV).

"Though the fig tree does not bud and there are no grapes on the vines ... yet I will rejoice in the Lord, I will be joyful in God my Savior" (Habakkuk 3:17-18, NIV).

"The Lord is close to the brokenhearted and saves those who are crushed in spirit" (Psalm 34:18, NIV).

Chapter 9

What It Means to Follow the Truth
The Call to Surrender

Dear Truthseeker,

Following the Truth isn't a one-time decision; it's a daily surrender. It's not simply saying "yes" once and moving on. It's waking up each day and choosing again, choosing to live by what is eternal, rather than what is easy. The temporal often looks easier, less costly, and more comfortable, but cannot satisfy. Truth calls us deeper, beyond the comfort of what fades, into the strength of what endures.

It's a commitment to walk in the light, even when the world celebrates the dark. To stand anchored in what is unshakable when everything around us feels uncertain.

When Jesus said, "Follow Me," He wasn't offering a path of convenience, but a call to transformation. He calls us to leave behind the old ways, to let go of the lies we've believed, and to step into the freedom of His light. Following Him means dying to self, comfort, control—and in that surrender, discovering the only way to truly live.

The invitation is both costly and beautiful: to lose what cannot last so that you may gain what cannot be taken away.

Truth is not just something you believe, He is someone you follow.

And Jesus never said, "Come believe in Me and stay the same."

He said, *"Follow Me."* Leave the old. Let go of the lies. Come and die to self, to comfort, to control and live.

> *"If anyone wants to follow after Me, let him deny himself, take up his cross daily, and follow Me"* (Luke 9:23, CSB).

To follow the Truth means you no longer lead your own life. God makes us most ourselves, but that self comes through surrender. Always surrender first, then a sense of self; of Real Being. I'd say death to false self is the way of knowing one's self in Christ.

You don't follow your feelings.

You don't follow the crowd.

You don't follow the culture.

You follow **Christ.** Its loss and victory, simultaneously, just like Jesus on the cross.

It's not always popular. It's not always easy.

But it is always worth it.

The Most Excellent Way
Obedience to Jesus may sound like loss to the world, but in the Kingdom, it's the pathway to **freedom**. It's not a performance for approval; it's a response to love.

You don't follow Truth to earn God's love.

You follow because **you already have it**.

And that love, the kind that doesn't flinch at your mess, doesn't abandon you in your doubt, and doesn't keep a record of wrongs is the most excellent way.

> *"And now I will show you the most excellent way"*
> (1 Corinthians 12:31, NIV).

> *"Love is patient, love is kind ... it always protects, always trusts, always hopes, always perseveres. Love never fails"* (1 Corinthians 13:4-8, NLT).

This is the love that transforms obedience from duty into desire.

When Scripture speaks of the love of Christ, it isn't describing a surface-level feeling, it's a transforming love that reaches into our deepest desires. Left on our own, our wants are often tangled with selfishness, comfort, or control. But when we encounter His love, something shifts. Suddenly, obedience is no longer about checking boxes, keeping rules, or living under pressure. Instead, His love reshapes what we long for at the core.

"This is the love that transforms obedience from duty into desire." His love takes obedience from being a burdensome "ought to" into a joyful "want to." Paying attention to our deep desires matters because they reveal what we believe will satisfy us. When those desires are aligned with Christ's love, they are not suppressed or denied, they are purified, reordered, and honored. We discover that what we truly want most is not against God, but fulfilled in Him.

In this way, obedience isn't about ignoring what we want but about allowing Christ's love to refine and elevate our desires so that what we want and what He wants become the same.

This is the love that:
- Leads you when the path is unclear.
- Lifts you when shame tries to silence you.
- Listens to your questions without withdrawing.
- Liberates you from the lies of performance and perfectionism.

Following the Truth means you're not following rules, you're following a **Person** Who laid down His life for you. And in doing so, He laid out a new way of life:
> The way of mercy.
> The way of truth.
> The way of love.
> The most excellent way.

You were never meant to follow from a distance.
You were meant to walk in step with Him, guided by His voice, grounded in His Word, and gripped by His love.

This kind of love doesn't just rescue you from sin.

It **reshapes** you.

It reorders your priorities.

It redefines your purpose.

And it releases you to love others in the same radical way He first loved you.

The Cost, and the Beauty of Following
No one accidentally follows Jesus. It's a conscious choice, a costly one. It means walking away from things the world celebrates. It means laying down your rights, your reputation, and sometimes your relationships.

Jesus said it plainly:
> *"Whoever does not carry their cross and follow me cannot be my disciple"* (Luke 14:27, NIV).

Following Jesus will cost you something. But not following Him will cost you *everything*.

Because there is no life outside of Him. There is no truth, no purpose, no peace, only an endless chase for counterfeit answers that never satisfy. The cross isn't just a symbol of death. It's the door to *resurrection life, a*nd that's the beauty of it.

When you surrender to Him, really surrender, you don't lose yourself. You find yourself.

You come alive to what's real. You're no longer defined by what's behind you, but by the One Who went before you. You may carry scars, but they don't disqualify you. They remind you that grace met you in the fire and brought you through.

> *When you surrender to Him, really surrender, you don't lose yourself. You find yourself.*

That's the paradox of the Gospel:
You die ... and yet, you finally live.

> *"I have been crucified with Christ and I no longer live, but Christ lives in me. The life I now live in the body, I live by faith in the Son of God, who loved me and gave himself for me"* (Galatians 2:20, CSB).

Dear one, following the Truth may strip away the false comforts you've leaned on, but it will clothe you in something eternal.

His love is not cheap. But it is freely given. And it's worth everything

Personal Challenge to the Truthseeker
Take inventory of your current walk with Jesus. Are you following at a distance or walking closely in step with Him? Identify one area where comfort, fear, or convenience may be keeping you from fully surrendering. This week, take one step toward deeper obedience, whether that means saying yes to something He's calling you into or letting go of something He's asking you to release.

Prayer

Jesus,

I want to follow You, not just with words, but with my life. Teach me to walk in Your truth when it's inconvenient, costly, or lonely. Show me what it means to take up my cross daily and follow You in love, not fear. Strip away every false version of truth I've clung to, and replace it with Your voice, Your peace, and Your presence. I choose to trust You, even when the way is narrow, because You are the way.
Amen.

Journal Prompt

• Where in your life is Jesus asking you to follow Him more fully?

_____

_____

_____

_____

_____

_____

_____

• What would change if you truly believed His way is the most excellent way?

_____

_____

_____

_____

_____

_____

_____

• How can you reflect His love more clearly in your obedience?

_____

_____

_____

_____

_____

_____

_____

Scripture Reflection

"If you love me, you will keep my commandments" (John 14:15, ESV).

"Follow God's example, therefore, as dearly loved children and walk in the way of love, just as Christ loved us ..." (Ephesians 5:1-2, NIV).

"Teach me your way, O Lord, that I may walk in your truth; unite my heart to fear your name" (Psalm 86:11, ESV).

Chapter 10

An Invitation to Come Home
The Heart of the Father

Dear Truthseeker,

You've made it this far not by accident, not by curiosity alone, but because the One Who *is* Truth has been drawing you the whole time.

This journey hasn't been about rules or religion. It's been about rescue. It's been about *coming home.* No matter where you've been, what you've believed, or how long you've been wandering, this moment is for you.

You're not too far gone.

You're not too broken.

You're not too late.

The God Who formed you, who's watched over you in every valley and whispered through every question, is still standing at the door.

> *"See! I stand at the door and knock. If anyone hears My voice and opens the door, I will come in ..."*
> (Revelation 3:20, NKJV).

He's not waiting to punish you.

He's waiting to embrace you.

This isn't just an invitation to believe something, it's a call to *belong*. To step into relationship with Jesus, Who is the Way, the Truth, and the Life.

> *"Come to Me, all who are weary and burdened, and I will give you rest"* (Matthew 11:28, NKJV).

This is your moment. Your turning point.

Not the end of your search, but the beginning of your story.

The Call to Say Yes
What you feel tugging at your heart right now isn't pressure, it's an invitation. The weight you feel is the weight of glory, not guilt. It's the Holy Spirit saying *this is it. You don't have to keep running. You don't have to keep fixing. Come home.*

Coming home to Jesus is not about having all the answers.

It's about trusting the One Who *is* the Answer.

It's not about being clean enough, it's about letting the Blood of Jesus make you new.

It's not about religion. It's about *relationship* with the living God.

He already made the first move. He sent His Son to die in your place so you could live.

> *"For God so loved the world, that He gave His one and only Son, that whoever believes in Him shall not perish but have eternal life"* (John 3:16,NKJV).

He's not waiting for perfection.

He's waiting for a **yes**.

A Salvation Prayer - Your Response To the Invitation

Jesus,

I hear You calling me, and I say, "Yes."

I believe you are the Son of God. I believe you died and rose again for me.

I turn from my sin, and I turn toward You.

Forgive me. Wash me. Make me new.

I give You my past, my pain, my striving, and my shame.

I receive Your love, Your mercy, and Your truth.

Fill me with Your Holy Spirit.

Teach me to follow You, to walk in Your Word, and to live in the fullness of Your truth.

From this day on, I belong to You.

I am Yours.

Amen.

If you just prayed that prayer, heaven is rejoicing and so am I.

Whether this is your new journey or you are already a follower of Christ, we begin this journey of becoming, not perfect, but whole, anchored in Truth, and carried by grace.

Personal Challenge to the Truthseeker
This week, take one bold step of alignment with the Truth you've now received. Whether it's joining a local church, opening the Bible daily, or confessing truth to someone you trust, *act on what God is doing in your heart.* Faith without movement remains dormant, but faith in motion where is freedom starts to flourish.

Ask the Lord this question:
"Now that I've said yes, what would You have me do next?"

Then listen. He will lead you.

> *"In all your ways acknowledge Him, and He will direct your paths"* (Proverbs 3:6, NKJV).

Journal Prompt
• What does "coming home" to God mean to you personally?

_____
_____
_____
_____
_____
_____
_____
_____
_____

• Reflect on the moments in your life where you felt far from God. What made you feel distant? What is He showing you now about His nearness?

_____

_____

_____

_____

_____

_____

_____

_____

_____

_____

_____

• What will change in your life now that you've said yes to Truth?

_____

_____

_____

_____

_____

_____

_____

_____

_____

_____

_____

_____

_____

• What is your response if He is saying to you like he said to me, "I just want you to get to KNOW me."

Let this be a space where you don't filter or edit just pour your heart out. Even your mess is welcome in His presence.

_____

_____

_____

_____

_____

_____

_____

_____

_____

_____

Scripture Reflection
"I have no greater joy than to hear that my children are walking in the truth" (3 John 1:4, NKJV).

"For the Son of Man came to seek and to save the lost" (Luke 19:10, NKJV).

'"You will seek me and find me when you seek me with all your heart. I will be found by you,' declares the Lord" (Jeremiah 29:13-14a, NKJV).

We find Him because He first found us!

Final Words to the Truthseeker
You didn't stumble here by accident. Every page, every tear, every wrestle with Truth, it's all been part of His pursuit of your heart.

This is not the end.

This is the *beginning*.

You were made to walk with God.

You were made to live in truth.

You were made to bring others into the light you've found.

Let this book be the spark.

Let your life be the fire.
You are deeply loved.

You are not alone.

You are home.

With all my heart,
Your fellow Truthseeker

Next Steps: Walking Out the Truth
So, you've said, "Yes," to Jesus. Now what?

Here are some foundational steps to help you grow, stay grounded, and walk forward in truth. Do not make this a ritual and a religious activity. It is relational and a conversation with Him. It will look different for each of us, so lean into His voice daily and let Him lead the process.

Mine looks like this: Every day in my journal, when I sit with Him, I ask, "Holy Spirit, what are Father and Jesus saying to me today?"

1. Talk to God Every Day
Prayer doesn't have to be formal, just honest. Speak to Him like a Father, a friend, a Savior. He listens.

2. Read the Bible Daily
Start with the Gospel of John to learn more about Jesus. Let God's Word become your source of truth and direction.

3. Find a Local, Bible-Teaching Church
Community is essential. You were never meant to walk alone. Surround yourself with believers who will encourage and disciple you.

4. Get Baptized
Baptism is a public declaration of the new life you've received. It's a powerful next step in your journey.

5. Tell Someone
Share what God has done in you. There is power in your testimony, and your story can spark faith in someone else.

Resources
Here are a few tools and recommendations to help you grow in your walk:

Bibles:
Be led to what translation brings alive His Word in your heart. He will lead you, but you can start with these:
- *YouVersion Bible App* (Free and includes reading plans)
- *NLT Life Application Study Bible*

Books
- *New Morning Mercies* by Paul David Tripp
- *Emotionally Healthy Spirituality* by Pete Scazzero
- *Experience Jesus. Really.* by John Eldridge

Podcasts & Teachers
- *The Bible Project* (podcast & videos)
- *The Bible Recap* – Tara-Leigh Cobble
- *The Gospel Truth* – Andrew Wommack

Discipleship Tools
- *Alpha Course*
- *Rooted Discipleship Program* (Check with local churches)

ABOUT THE AUTHOR

Grace Emma Abbey is a passionate teacher, US Army Reserve Chaplain, and ministry leader dedicated to helping others discover truth, healing, and hope in Christ. She provides spiritual care, counseling, and guidance to soldiers and students. As a ministry leader her life and writing reflect a deep passion for truth, healing, and spiritual formation.

With a Master of Divinity from The King's University and over fifteen years of ministry experience, Grace has led prayer movements, counseled leaders, and served in local and national ministry settings. She is the founder and director of Mansfield House of Prayer, now called The House of Prayer—DFW, a ministry dedicated to intercession, experiencing Jesus intimately, discipleship, and community transformation.

Grace's story begins with her parents, who first introduced her to the love and presence of God. Growing up surrounded by a faith-filled family in Ghana, she learned early the power of prayer, perseverance, and community. Those formative years continue to shape her heart for people, her compassion in ministry, and her belief that true hope is found only in Christ.

Beyond her professional and ministry work, Grace finds her greatest joy in being a mother to her daughter, Kamillah, whose creativity and faith continue to inspire her. Her formation as a leader and writer has been deeply shaped by a safe community of friends—a circle of faith-filled companions who have prayed with her, stood with her through seasons of growth, healing, calling, and encouraged her to live authentically in God's truth.

Grace lives by 1 Corinthians 13:4–8 and is known for reminding herself and others with bold joy: *"The devil is a LIAR!"*

In *Dear Truthseeker*, Grace writes with conviction and compassion, from a place of authenticity and grace, inviting readers to wrestle honestly with life's questions to find freedom, peace, and purpose in the unchanging truth of Jesus Christ. Most of all, to invite readers to encounter the Truth, Himself—Jesus Christ.

www.ingramcontent.com/pod-product-compliance
Lightning Source LLC
LaVergne TN
LVHW051809080426
835513LV00017B/1872